W9-AGU-609

Up, Up, and Away

by Anne Cambal

PEARSON

Scott
Foresman

Editorial Offices: Glenview, Illinois • Parsippany, New Jersey • New York, New York
Sales Offices: Needham, Massachusetts • Duluth, Georgia • Glenview, Illinois
Coppell, Texas • Ontario, California • Mesa, Arizona

Every effort has been made to secure permission and provide appropriate credit for photographic material. The publisher deeply regrets any omission and pledges to correct errors called to its attention in subsequent editions.

Unless otherwise acknowledged, all photographs are the property of Scott Foresman, a division of Pearson Education.

Photo locators denoted as follows: Top (T), Center (C), Bottom (B), Left (L), Right (R), Background (Bkgd)

Opener: NASA, Associated Press, Getty Images; 1 NASA/Glen Research Center; 3 Getty Image, Library of Congress; 4 ©DK Images; 5 ©DK Images; 6 Getty Images, Corbis; 7 Corbis; 8 Library of Congress; 9 Library of Congress; 10 ©DK Images; 11 ©DK Images; 12 ©DK Images; 13 Corbis; 14 NASA/Glen Research Center; 17 Associated Press; 18 ©DK Images; 20 NASA; 22 Getty Images; 23 NASA

ISBN: 0-328-13497-X

Copyright © Pearson Education, Inc.

All Rights Reserved. Printed in the United States of America. This publication is protected by Copyright, and permission should be obtained from the publisher prior to any prohibited reproduction, storage in a retrieval system, or transmission in any form by any means, electronic, mechanical, photocopying, recording, or likewise. For information regarding permission(s), write to: Permissions Department, Scott Foresman, 1900 East Lake Avenue, Glenview, Illinois 60025.

7 8 9 10 V0G1 14 13 12 11 10 09 08

Aviation

The word *aviation* refers to the science of flight. Today, people fly in such heavier-than-air aircraft as helicopters, airplanes, gliders, and space shuttles, or they can soar in lighter-than-air aircraft, such as hot-air balloons.

Modern aviation can be divided into three broad areas. Commercial aviation includes passenger planes and helicopters. Military aviation includes a wide range of aircraft such as fighter planes. General aviation includes flying for sport and flying instruction.

The flight of the Wright brothers at Kitty Hawk, North Carolina, on December 17, 1903, came about through hard work and ingenuity, or know-how. Their work was influenced by those who came before them. Other inventors, soldiers, business people, and dreamers, who first began to explore flight, helped the Wright brothers. The success of the Wright brothers came about through years of observing and experimenting.

This is one of Orville and Wilbur Wright's gliders.

Forces and Famous Names

An airplane is a craft that is heavier than air, but that can still fly. For it to lift off, several forces must be working for and against the aircraft. Gravity, lift, thrust, wind, and **drag** are the forces that affect an airplane in flight. Gravity, or weight, pulls down on a plane. Lift, which happens when air is moving over and under a plane's wing, helps push a plane upward. Thrust, caused by either the plane's moving propeller or by a jet engine, pushes the airplane forward. Drag is the air, or wind, that resists the airplane's forward motion and slows the airplane down.

Different forces help a plane take to the sky.

Leonardo da Vinci (1452–1519) designed an ornithopter, a flying machine based on how birds fly. The rider's arms and legs powered the machine by flapping the wings. Da Vinci also designed a propeller and a parachute.

Eighteenth-century French inventors, Joseph-Michel and Jacques-Étienne Montgolfier, had ideas too. They designed and built the first practical hot-air balloon.

Sir George Cayley (1773–1857) has been called the Father of Modern Aviation. Experimenting with kites and a **glider,** or an aircraft without an engine, he formulated the basic principles of heavier-than-air flying.

The Montgolfier brothers constructed a hot-air balloon.

Felix du Temple de la Croix (1823–1890) made history as the first person to fly a powered airplane. The problem was that it only worked when flying downhill.

Wilbur (1867–1912) and Orville (1871–1948) Wright made history. Their plane did not **stall** and stop. Theirs was the first sustained flight in a powered airplane.

Sometimes inventions come about through the help of other inventors' ideas, and one inventor's idea can spark another inventor's idea. The writings and work of Otto Lilienthal (1848–1896) inspired the work of the Wright brothers. Lilienthal had developed more than a dozen different models of hang gliders, and he thought that flying was everything.

Glen Curtiss (1878–1930) first flew in 1908. He flew *White Wing,* an aircraft produced by a group of scientists. Over the next several years, he set distance records in America and Europe. He is best known for his design of the seaplane and the flying boat, a large seaplane that carried passengers. The first successful takeoff from a U.S. Navy ship happened with a Curtiss plane. Curtiss also built the Triad, the first U.S. Navy aircraft.

(Left to right) Otto Lilienthal, Glen Curtiss, and the Wright brothers

Charles Lindbergh (1902–1974) is best known as the first person to fly nonstop from New York City to Paris. He made this flight in 1927. A Wright brothers engine powered his plane, the *Spirit of St. Louis.*

Amelia Earhart (1897–1937) flew her plane across the Atlantic five years after Lindbergh. Her flight set several flying records. She was the first woman to fly solo across the Atlantic and the first person to fly across the Atlantic twice—her first trip was as a passenger.

Olive Ann Beech (1903–1993) is known as "The First Lady of Aviation." Olive and her husband Walter founded Beech Aircraft in 1932. They ran the company together until Walter died in 1950, and then Olive ran Beech Aircraft for nearly twenty more years. The Gemini and Apollo space missions, as well as other space shuttle missions, used Beech airplane parts and products.

Charles Lindbergh and the *Spirit of St. Louis*

AMELIA EARHART
World's Premiere Aviatrix

Appearing Personally to Tell Her Story of Aviation
"Flying for Fun"

Printed in U. S. A.

Amelia Earhart

Ballooning

What is it that makes a hot-air balloon fly? The idea behind hot-air balloons is this: Hot air rises and cold air falls. The heated air in a hot-air balloon makes it rise.

The three parts of a hot-air balloon are the basket, the burner, and the envelope. Passengers ride in the basket, a kind of **cradle** commonly made of wicker. The basket must be light and able to bend and **flex.** There's very little room in the basket. Some are a snug fit for two, while others are designed to hold ten or more people.

The wicker basket holds
hot-air balloon passengers.

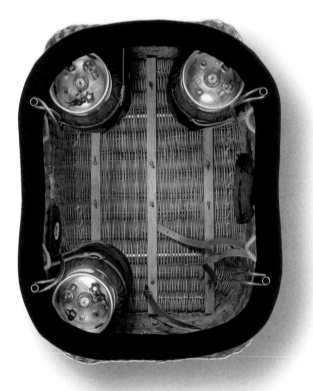

This container holds propane gas.

This is how a hot-air balloon is inflated before lifting off.

The burner creates a large flame by burning liquid propane gas. This heats the air inside the envelope, or balloon, which is often made of colorful fabric. When the air inside the balloon is heated, it becomes warmer than the air outside it. Because the air inside the balloon is warmer than the air outside it, it is also lighter. This makes the balloon rise. To descend, the pilot adjusts the burner to cool the air in the balloon. Balloon pilots might use liquefied propane gas in the form of mist when flying over farms. It is quieter to burn than gas, so it does not scare the animals!

A hot-air balloon goes where the wind takes it, so the pilot doesn't know exactly where the aircraft will fly. Before taking off, however, the pilot studies the weather reports, paying close attention to the wind currents. A hot-air balloon cannot be steered like a car, ship, or airplane. There's no steering wheel, such as in a car, or **rudder,** as in a ship or airplane, to help control the movement of a balloon. The pilot can, however, choose which layer of air the balloon will ride on. Different layers of air can blow in different directions. Some days a pilot can head the balloon in only one direction, and other days he or she can go forward and back. It all depends on the winds.

The balloon rises and takes flight.

The hot-air balloon is inflated with hot air.

While a balloon is in flight, a group called the chase crew is working hard. The chase crew follows the balloon in a chase vehicle. The crew stays in radio contact with the pilot during flight and meets the balloon where it lands. When possible, the crew also communicates with the owner of the land where the balloon sets down. This helps ensure that the landing is smooth and safe. Finally, the crew helps pack up the balloon and transports it to a **hangar,** where it will be stored.

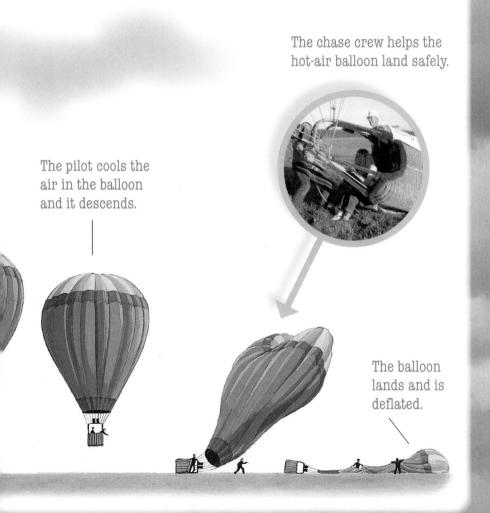

The chase crew helps the hot-air balloon land safely.

The pilot cools the air in the balloon and it descends.

The balloon lands and is deflated.

Balloon Festivals

Balloon clubs and festivals are popular around the world. The Balloon Sport Club Tokyo sails every weekend in Watarase, a town about 60 kilometers (37 miles), from Tokyo, Japan. In England, balloon festivals in Northampton and Southampton bring tourists and participants from around the world. The International Balloon Festival of Saint-Jean-sur-Richelieu is the biggest balloon festival in Canada. Canada also holds the Gatineau Hot-Air Balloon Festival in Quebec.

The world's largest ballooning event is the Albuquerque, New Mexico, International Balloon Fiesta. This has been held yearly since 1972. Beginning with only thirteen balloons, this festival has grown to more than nine hundred balloons and more than one thousand pilots. More than a million people have watched the festivities.

Albuquerque is an excellent location for ballooning. The combination of mountains, wind currents, and long vistas make it ideal for the crews and the tourists alike.

People around the world enjoy balloon festivals.

Ballooning Achievements

In recent years, many time and distance records have been set in ballooning.

1997: Steve Fossett was not able to complete a trip around the world in his balloon, *Solo Spirit*. He did, however, set the record for the greatest distance: 16,602 kilometers (10,361 miles).

1999: Brian Jones and Bertrand Piccard were the first to pilot a balloon around the world. The March flight took 19 days, 13 hours, and covered almost 41,000 kilometers (25,000 miles).

This balloon flies in cold weather.

2000: David Hempleman-Adams set three new balloon records in a single flight. He is the first balloonist to fly solo over the Arctic Ocean. He set a new British duration record. He flew for 132 hours. Adams also flew closer to the North Pole than anyone else.

2002: Heidrun Prosch set an altitude record as a female balloonist. Her balloon soared 10,773 meters (35,344 feet) into the sky over Austria.

Even after a hundred years of aircraft, there are still new regions to explore and records to be set!

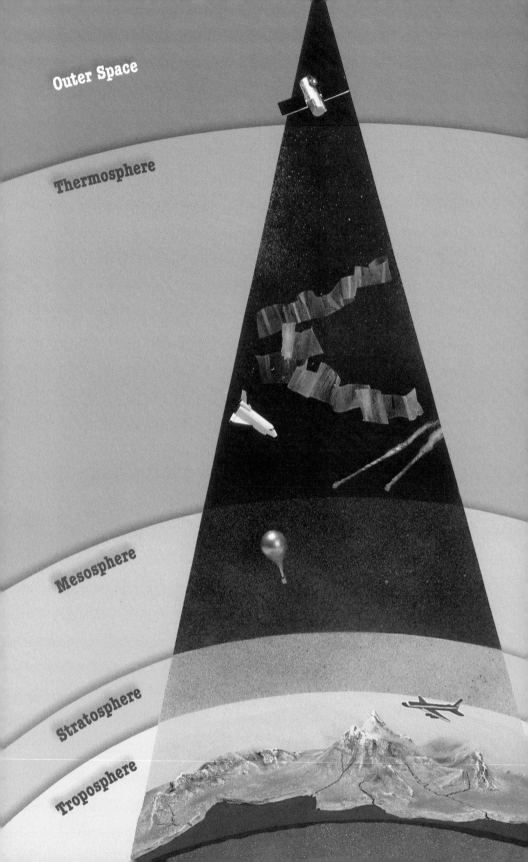

Outer Space

Thermosphere

Mesosphere

Stratosphere

Troposphere

Earth's Atmosphere

Earth's atmosphere is made up of all the air that is around the planet. It extends from the water and the ground, all the way up to deep space. Several different layers make up the atmosphere. Each one has a name and its own characteristics, or qualities. There are no specific boundaries between these layers because the changes are gradual.

The atmosphere is made up of gases, mostly oxygen and nitrogen. The amounts and the mixture change from layer to layer. It is only in the lowest layer where these gases support life. This layer is called the *troposphere,* where we live. It extends for only 16 kilometers (10 miles). Scientists also refer to this layer as the lower atmosphere.

The next layer up is called the *stratosphere.* This layer is dryer than the troposphere and not as dense, or thick. The lower part of this layer is very cold. The temperature is about –57°C (–70°F). Water freezes at 0°C (32°F), so that's cold! The rest of the stratosphere is warmer. At the very top—40 kilometers (about 25 miles) above Earth—the temperature can reach –15°C (5°F). Also, the ozone layer is found in the stratosphere. The ozone layer absorbs harmful ultraviolet rays from the sun.

Earth's atmosphere is made up of several different layers.

The next atmospheric layer is called the *mesosphere*. This layer reaches about 81 kilometers (50 miles) above planet Earth. The higher you go in this layer, the colder the temperature becomes. It can be as cold as –120°C (–184°F) in the upper mesosphere. Together, the stratosphere and the mesosphere make up what scientists call the middle atmosphere. These layers are between the troposphere and the final atmospheric layer, which is called the *thermosphere*.

This is a view of Earth's atmosphere from outer space (below). This device gathers information that scientists use to study the Earth's atmosphere (right).

The thermosphere is the uppermost layer of the atmosphere, or the upper atmosphere. Here, temperatures rise to extremely hot levels as you go higher and higher up. In this layer, the temperature can be as high as 1,982°C (3,600°F). Keep in mind that water boils at 100°C (212°F), in comparison. Energy from the sun causes this huge temperature increase. Amazingly, this layer would feel very cold because the air is too thin to heat our skin.

The Jet Stream

The troposphere is the layer in which we live. It is also the layer of Earth's atmosphere where we experience weather. Within the troposphere is the jet stream. This can be thought of as a river of air, with an average speed of around 90 miles per hour. Earth has five or six major jet streams circling it. The position of the jet stream varies from day to day, and it affects how hot or cold and how wet or dry the weather will be.

Scientists study the jet stream to predict the weather. Pilots and airplane passengers rely on accurate wind and weather forecasts for safe flights, and aircraft pilots plan their routes based on these forecasts. On one flight, an aircraft might benefit from a strong jet stream on its tail. Another time, it may take more fuel to travel the same distance because of oncoming winds.

Some jet streams are related to the cold air of the North and South Poles. Others are named for the warm air of the tropics near the equator. In all cases, these strong currents push cold or hot air, and everything else associated with weather, around the globe. A jet stream blowing over any part of the world can change the weather in that area.

Pilots depend on accurate weather forecasts.

Meteorologists will continue to study the jet stream to predict the weather, and pilots will continue to depend on their forecasts. Through flight, we will continue to take to the sky and beyond.

This view of a jet stream was taken from space.

Glossary

cradle *n.* a frame to support weight.

drag *n.* the force acting on an object in motion, in a direction opposite to the object's motion.

flex *v.* to bend.

glider *n.* an aircraft without an engine.

hangar *n.* a building for storing aircraft.

rudder *n.* a flat piece of wood or metal hinged vertically to the rear end of a ship or an aircraft and used to steer it.

stall *v.* stop or to bring to a standstill.